The Extra Big 'N' Extra Crunchy Captain Underpants Book O' Fun

Dav Pilkey

Scholastic Children's Books
An imprint of Scholastic Ltd
Euston House, 24 Eversholt Street
London, NW1 1DB, UK
Registered office: Westfield Road, Southam,
Warwickshire, CV47 0RA
SCHOLASTIC and associated logos are trademarks and
or registered trademarks of Scholastic Inc.

The Adventures of Captain Underpants
First published in the US by Scholastic Inc., 1997
Copyright © Dav Pilkey, 1997

The Captain Underpants Extra-Crunchy Book O' Fun
First published in the US by Scholastic Inc., 2001
Copyright © Dav Pilkey, 2001

The All New Captain Underpants Extra-Crunchy Book O' Fun 2
First published in the US by Scholastic Inc., 2002
Copyright © Dav Pilkey, 2002

This edition published in the UK by Scholastic Ltd, 2008

The right of Dav Pilkey to be identified as the author and illustrator
of this work has been asserted by him.

10 digit ISBN 1 407 10529 9
13 digit ISBN 978 1407 10529 1

British Library Cataloguing-in-Publication Data
A CIP catalogue record for this book is available from the British Library

Printed by Bookmarque Ltd, Croydon, Surrey
Papers used by Scholastic Children's Books are made
from wood grown in sustainable forests.

7 9 10 8

www.scholastic.co.uk/zone

CHAPTER 1
GEORGE AND HAROLD

Meet George Beard and Harold Hutchins. George is
the kid on the left with the tie and the flat-top. Harold is
the one on the right with the T-shirt and the bad haircut.
Remember that now.

George and Harold were best friends. They had a lot in common. They lived right next door to each other and they were both in the same fourth-grade class at Jerome Horwitz Elementary School.

George and Harold were usually responsible kids. Whenever anything bad happened, George and Harold were usually responsible.

But don't get the wrong idea about these two. George and Harold were actually very nice boys. No matter what everybody else thought, they were good, sweet, and lovable… Well, OK, maybe they weren't so sweet and lovable, but they were good nonetheless.

It's just that George and Harold each had a "silly streak" a kilometre long. Usually that silly streak was hard to control. Sometimes it got them into trouble. And once it got them into big, BIG trouble.

But before I can tell you that story, I have to tell you this story.

CHAPTER 2
TREE HOUSE COMIX, INC.

After a hard day of cracking jokes, pulling pranks, and causing mayhem at school, George and Harold liked to rush to the old tree house in George's backyard. Inside the tree house were two big old fluffy chairs, a table, a cupboard crammed with junk food, and a padlocked crate filled with pencils, pens and stacks and stacks of paper.

Now, Harold loved to draw, and George loved to make up stories. And together, the two boys spent hours and hours writing and drawing their very own comic books.

Over the years, they had created hundreds of their own comics, starring dozens of their own superheroes. First there was "Dog Man", then came "Timmy the Talking Toilet", and who could forget "The Amazing Cow Lady"?

But the all-time greatest superhero they ever made up *had* to be "The Amazing Captain Underpants".

George came up with the idea.

"Most superheroes *look* like they're flying around in their underwear," he said. "Well, this guy actually *is* flying around in his underwear!"

The two boys laughed and laughed.

"Yeah," said Harold, "he could fight with *Wedgie Power*!"

George and Harold spent entire afternoons writing and drawing the comic adventures of Captain Underpants. He was their coolest superhero ever!

Luckily for the boys, the secretary at Jerome Horwitz Elementary School was much too busy to keep an eye on the photocopier. So whenever they got a chance, Harold and George would sneak into the office and run off several hundred copies of their latest Captain Underpants adventure.

After school, they sold their homemade comics on the playground for 50¢ each.

CHAPTER 3
THE ADVENTURES OF
CAPTAIN UNDERPANTS

Written By George Beard

Cartoons By Harold Hutchins

CHAPTER 4
MEAN OLD MR KRUPP

Do you see that old guy looking out of the window up there? That's Mr Krupp, the principal.

Now, Mr Krupp was the meanest,
sourest old principal in the whole history of Jerome
Horwitz Elementary School. He hated laughter and
singing. He hated the sounds of children playing at
break-time. In fact, he hated children altogether!

And guess which two children Mr Krupp hated most of all?

If you guessed George and Harold, you're right! Mr Krupp *hated* George and Harold.

He hated their pranks and their wisecracks. He hated their silly attitudes and their constant giggling. And he especially hated those awful *Captain Underpants* comic books.

"I'm going to get those boys one day," Mr Krupp vowed. "One day very, very soon!"

CHAPTER 5
ONE DAY VERY, VERY SOON

Remember when I said that George and Harold's "silly streak" got them into big, *BIG* trouble once? Well, this is the story of how that happened. And how some huge pranks (and a little blackmail) turned their principal into the coolest superhero of all time.

It was the day of the big football game between the Horwitz Knuckleheads and the Stubinville Stinkbugs. The stands were packed with fans.

JEROME HORWITZ ELEMENTARY

SEE OUR BIG FOOTBALL GAME *TODAY*

The cheerleaders ran on to the field and shook their pom-poms over their heads.

A fine black dust drifted out of their pom-poms and settled all around them.

"Gimme a K!" shouted the cheerleaders.

"K !" repeated the fans.

"Gimme an N!" shouted the cheerleaders.

"N !" repeated the fans.

"Gimme an . . . a-ah-ah-A-CHOO!" sneezed the cheerleaders.

"A-ah-ah-A-CHOO!" repeated the fans.

The cheerleaders sneezed and sneezed
and sneezed some more. They couldn't stop sneezing.
"Hey!" shouted a fan in the stands. "Somebody sprinkled black pepper into the cheerleaders' pom-poms!"
"I wonder who did that?" asked another fan.

The cheerleaders stumbled off the field, sneezing and dripping with mucus, as the marching band members took their places.

But when the band began to play, steady streams of bubbles began blowing out of their instruments! Bubbles were *everywhere*! Up and down the field the marching band slipped and slid, leaving behind a thick trail of wet, bubbly foam.

"Hey!" shouted a fan in the stands. "Somebody poured bubble bath into the marching band's instruments!"

"I wonder who did that?" asked another fan.

A-CHOO
ACHOOO

Soon, the football teams took the field. The Knuckleheads kicked the ball. Up, up, up went the ball. Higher and higher it went. The ball sailed into the clouds and kept right on going until nobody could see it any more.

"Hey!" shouted a fan in the stands. "Somebody filled the game ball with *helium*!"

"I wonder who did that?" asked another fan.

But the missing ball didn't make any
difference because at that moment, the Knuckleheads
were rolling around the field, scratching and itching like
crazy.

"Hey!" shouted the coach. "Somebody replaced our
Deep-Heating Muscle Rub Lotion with Mr Prankster's
Extra-Scratchy Itching Cream!"

"We wonder who did that?!" shouted the fans in the
stands.

The whole afternoon went on much the same way, with people shouting everything from "Hey, somebody put Sea-Monkeys in the lemonade!" to "Hey, somebody glued all the bathroom doors shut!"

Before long, most of the fans in the stands had left. The big game had been forfeited, and everyone in the entire school was *miserable*.

Everyone, that is, except for two giggling boys crouching in the shadows beneath the stands.

"Those were our best pranks yet!" laughed Harold.

"Yep," chuckled George, "they'll be hard to top, that's for sure."

"I just hope we don't get busted for this," said Harold.

"Don't worry," said George. "We covered our tracks really well. There's *no way* we'll get busted!"

32

CHAPTER 6
BUSTED

The next day at school, an announcement came over the loudspeakers.

"George Beard and Harold Hutchins, please report to Principal Krupp's office at once."

"Uh-oh!" said Harold. "I don't like the sound of *that*!"
"Don't worry," said George. "They can't prove any-thing!"

George and Harold entered Principal Krupp's office and sat down on the chairs in front of his desk. The two boys had been in this office together countless times before, but this time was different. Mr Krupp was *smiling*. As long as George and Harold had known Mr Krupp, they had never, *ever* seen him smile. Mr Krupp knew something.

"I didn't see you boys at the big game yesterday," said Mr Krupp.

"Uh, no," said George. "We weren't feeling well."

"Y-Y-Yeah," Harold stammered nervously. "W-W-We went home."

"Aw, that's too bad," said Principal Krupp. "You boys missed a good game."

George and Harold quickly glanced at each other, gulped, and tried hard not to look guilty.

"Lucky for you, I have a videotape of the whole thing," Mr Krupp said. He turned on the television in the corner and pressed the play button on the VCR.

A black-and-white image appeared on the TV screen.
It was an overhead shot of George and Harold sprinkling
pepper into the cheerleaders' pom-poms. Next came a
shot of George and Harold pouring liquid bubble bath
into the marching band's instruments.

"How do you like the *pre-game show*?" asked Mr
Krupp with a devilish grin.

George eyed the television screen in terror. He couldn't answer. Harold's eyes were glued to the floor. He couldn't look.

The tape went on and on, revealing all of George and Harold's "behind the scenes" antics. By now, both boys were eyeing the floor, squirming nervously, and dripping with sweat.

Mr Krupp turned off the TV.

"You know," he said, "ever since you boys came to this school, it's been one prank after another. First you put dissected frogs in the salad at the parent-teacher banquet. Then you made it snow in the cafeteria. Then you rigged all the intercoms so they played "Weird Al" Yankovic songs *full blast* for six hours straight.

"For *four long years* you two have been running amok in this school, and I've never been able to prove anything – until now!"

Mr Krupp held the videotape in his hand. "I took the liberty of installing tiny video surveillance cameras all around the school. I knew I'd catch you two in the act one day. I just didn't know it would be *so easy*!"

CHAPTER 7
A LITTLE BLACKMAIL

Mr Krupp sat back in his chair and chuckled to himself for a long, long time. Finally, George got up the courage to speak.

"W-What are you going to do with that tape?" he said.

"I thought you'd never ask," laughed Principal Krupp.

"I've thought long and hard about what to do with this tape," Mr Krupp said. "At first, I thought I'd send copies to your parents."

The boys swallowed hard and sank deeply into their chairs.

"Then I thought I might send a copy to the school board," Mr Krupp continued. "I could get you both *expelled* for this!"

The boys swallowed harder and sank deeper into their chairs.

"Finally, I came to a decision," Mr Krupp concluded. "I think the football team would be very curious to find out just *who* was responsible for yesterday's fiasco. I think I'll send a copy to them!"

George and Harold leaped out of their chairs and fell to their knees.

"No!" cried George. "You can't do that. They'll *kill* us!"

"Yeah," begged Harold, "they'll kill us every day for the rest of our lives!"

Mr Krupp laughed and laughed.

"Please have mercy," the boys cried. "We'll do anything!"

"Anything?" asked Principal Krupp with delight. He reached into his desk, pulled out a list of demands, and tossed it at the boys. "If you don't want to be *dead as long as you live*, you'll follow these rules *exactly*!"

George and Harold carefully looked over the list.
"This . . . this is blackmail!" said George.
"Call it what you like," Principal Krupp snapped, "but
if you two don't follow that list *exactly*, then this tape
becomes the property of the Horwitz Knuckleheads!"

RULES

#1. NO MORE PRACTICAL JOKES OR PRANKS

#2. NO LAUGHING OR SMILING

#3. NO MORE T

#4. NO MORE CAPTAIN UNDERPA

#5. WASH MY CAR EVER

#6. MOW MY

CHAPTER 8
CRIME AND PUNISHMENT

At six o'clock the next morning, George and Harold dragged themselves out of bed, walked over to Mr Krupp's house, and began washing his car.

Then, while Harold scrubbed the tyres, George roamed around the yard pulling up all the weeds and nettles he could find. Afterwards, they cleaned the gutters and washed all the windows on Mr Krupp's house.

At school, George and Harold sat up straight, listened carefully, and spoke only when spoken to. They didn't tell jokes, they didn't pull pranks – they didn't even smile.

Their teacher kept pinching herself. "I just *know* this is a dream," she said.

At lunch, the two boys vacuumed Mr. Krupp's office, shined his shoes, and polished his desktop. At break, they clipped his fingernails and ironed his tie.

Each spare moment in the boys' daily schedule was spent catering to Mr Krupp's every whim.

After school, George and Harold mowed Mr Krupp's lawn, tended his garden, and began painting the front of his house. At sunset, Mr Krupp came outside and handed each boy a stack of books.

"Gentlemen," he said, "I've asked your teachers to give you *both* extra homework. Now go home, study hard, and I'll see you back here at six o'clock tomorrow morning. We've got a busy day ahead of us."

"Thank you, sir," moaned the two boys.

George and Harold walked home dead tired.

"Man, this was the worst day of my entire life," said George.

"Don't worry," said Harold. "We only have to do this for eight more years. Then we can move away to some far-off land where they'll never find us. Maybe Antarctica."

"I've got a better idea," said George.

He took a piece of paper out of his pocket and handed it to Harold. It was an old magazine ad for a 3-D Hypno-Ring.

"How's *this* going to help us?" asked Harold.

"All we gotta do is hypnotize Mr Krupp," said George. "We'll make him give us the video and forget this whole mess ever happened."

"That's a great idea!" said Harold. "And the best part is we only have to wait four-to-six weeks for delivery!"

CHAPTER 9
FOUR-TO-SIX
WEEKS LATER

After four-to-six weeks of backbreaking slave labour, gruelling homework assignments, and humiliating good behaviour at school, a package arrived in George's mailbox from the Li'l Wiseguy Novelty Company.

It was the 3-D Hypno-Ring.

"Hallelujah!" cried George. "It's everything I ever hoped for!"

"Let me see, let me see," said Harold.

"Don't look directly at it," warned George. "You don't want to get hypnotized, do you?"

"Do you really think it will work?" asked Harold. "Do you really think we can 'amaze our friends, control our enemies, and take over the world' just like the ad says?"

"It better work," said George. "Or else we've just wasted four whole bucks!"

CHAPTER 10
THE 3-D HYPNO-RING

The next morning, George and Harold didn't arrive early at Mr Krupp's house to wash his car and reshingle his roof. In fact, they were even a little late getting to school.

When they finally turned up, Mr Krupp was standing at the front door waiting for them. And boy, was he *angry*!

Mr Krupp escorted the boys into his office and slammed the door.

"All right, where were you two this morning?" he growled.

"We wanted to come over to your house," said George, "but we were busy trying to figure out the secret of this *ring*."

"What ring?" snapped Mr Krupp.

George held up his hand and showed the ring to Principal Krupp.

"It's got one of those weird patterns on it," said Harold. "If you stare at it long enough, a picture appears."

"Well, hold it still," snarled Mr Krupp. "I can't see the darn thing!"

"I have to move it back and forth," said George, "or else it won't work."

Mr Krupp's eyes followed the ring back and forth, back and forth, back and forth, and back and forth.

"You have to stare deeper into the ring," said Harold. "Deeper . . . deeeper . . . deeeeper . . . deeeeeeeeeper."

"You are getting sleepy," said George. "Veeeeery sleeeeeeeeeepy."

Mr Krupp's eyelids began to droop. "I'mmmsssooooosssleeepy," he mumbled.

After a few minutes, Mr Krupp's eyes were closed tight, and he began to snore.

"You are under our spell," said George. "When I snap my fingers, you will obey our every command!"

Snap!

"Iwwilllloobeyyy," mumbled Mr Krupp.

"All right," said George. "Have you still got that video-tape of me and Harold?"

"Yeeessss," mumbled Mr Krupp.

"Well, hand it over, bub," George instructed.

Mr Krupp unlocked a large filing cabinet and opened the bottom drawer. He reached in and handed George the videotape. George stuffed it into his backpack.

Harold took a *different* video out of his backpack and put it into the filing cabinet.

"What's that video?" asked George.

"It's one of my little sister's old 'Boomer the Purple Dragon Sing-A-Long' videos."

"Nice touch," said George.

CHAPTER 11
FUN WITH HYPNOSIS

When Harold bent down to close the filing cabinet, he took a quick look inside.

"Whoa!" he cried. "Look at all the stuff in here!"

The filing cabinet was filled with everything Mr Krupp had taken away from the boys over the years. There were slingshots, whoopee cushions, skateboards, fake doggy doo-doo – you name it, it was in there.

"Look at this!" cried George. "A big stack of *Captain Underpants* comics!"

"He's got every issue!" said Harold.

For hours, the two boys sat on the floor laughing and reading their comics. Finally, George looked up at the clock.

"Yikes!" he said. "It's almost lunchtime! We better clean up this mess and get to class."

The boys looked up at their principal, who had been standing behind them in a trance all morning.

"Gee, I almost forgot about Mr Krupp," said Harold. "What should we do with him?"

"Do you want to have some fun?" asked George.

"Why not?" said Harold. "I haven't had *any* fun in the last four-to-six weeks!"

"Cool," said George. He walked up to
Mr Krupp and snapped his fingers. *Snap!* "You are—a
chicken!" he said.

Suddenly, Mr Krupp leaped on to his desk and flapped
his arms. "Cluck, cluck, cluck-cluck," he cried, kicking
his papers off the desk behind him and pecking at his
pen-and-pencil set.

George and Harold howled with
laughter.

"Let me try, let me try," said Harold.

"Ummm, you are a – a *monkey*!"

"You gotta snap your fingers," said George.

"Oh, yeah," said Harold. *Snap!* "You are a *monkey*!"

Suddenly, Mr Krupp sprang off his desk and began swinging from the fluorescent light fixtures. "Ooo-ooo, ooo-oooo, OOOOO!" he shrieked, leaping from one side of the room to the other.

George and Harold laughed so hard they almost cried. "My turn, my turn!" said George. "Let's see. What should we turn him into next?"

"I know," Harold said, holding up a *Captain Underpants* comic. "Let's turn him into Captain Underpants!"

"Good idea," said George. *Snap!* "You are now the greatest superhero of all time: *The Amazing Captain Underpants*!"

Mr Krupp tore down the red curtain from his office window and tied it around his neck. Then he took off his shoes, socks, shirt, trousers and his awful toupee.

"Tra-La-Laaaaaaaa!" he sang.

Mr Krupp stood before them looking quite triumphant, with his cape blowing in the breeze of the open window. George and Harold were dumbfounded.

"You know," said George, "he kinda *looks* like Captain Underpants."

"Yeah," Harold replied.

After a short silence, the two boys looked at each other and burst into laughter. George and Harold had never laughed so hard in all their lives. Tears ran down their faces as they rolled about the floor, shrieking in hysterics.

After a while, George pulled himself up from the floor for another look.

"Hey," George cried. "Where'd he go?"

CHAPTER 12
OUT OF THE WINDOW

George and Harold dashed to the window and looked out. There, running across the car park, was a pudgy old guy in his underwear with a red cape flowing behind him.

TRA-LA-LAAA!

"Mr Krupp, come back!" shouted Harold.

"He won't answer to *that*," said George. "He thinks he's Captain Underpants now."

"Oh, no," said Harold.

"He's probably running off to fight crime," said George.

"Oh, *no,*" said Harold.

"And we gotta stop him," said George.

"Oh, NO," cried Harold. *"NO WAY!"*

"Look," said George, "he could get *killed* out there." Harold was unmoved.

"Or worse," said George. "We could get into BIG trouble!"

"You're right," said Harold. "We *gotta* go after him!"

The two boys opened the bottom cabinet drawer and took out their slingshots and skateboards.

"Do you think we should bring anything else?" asked Harold.

"Yeah," said George. "Let's bring the fake doggy doo-doo."

"Good thinking," said Harold. "You just never know when fake doggy doo-doo is going to come in handy!"

Harold stuffed Mr Krupp's clothes, shoes and toupee into his backpack. Then together the two boys leaped out of the window, slid down the flagpole, and took off on their skateboards after the Amazing Captain Underpants.

64

CHAPTER 13
BANK ROBBERS

George and Harold rode their skateboards all over town looking for Captain Underpants.

"I can't find him anywhere," said Harold.

"You'd think a guy like him would be *easy* to spot," said George.

Then the boys turned a corner, and *there* he was.
Captain Underpants – standing in front of a bank,
looking quite heroic.

"Mr Krupp!" cried Harold.

"Shhh," said George, "don't call him that. Call him
Captain Underpants!"

"Oh, yeah," said Harold.

"And don't forget to snap your fingers," said George.

"Right!" said Harold.

RRRRiiiiNNNG

ALARM

66

But before he got a chance, the bank doors flew wide open, and out stepped two robbers. The robbers took one look at Captain Underpants and stopped dead in their tracks.

"Surrender!" said Captain Underpants. "Or I will have to resort to *Wedgie Power*!"

"Oh, no," whispered Harold and George.

Nobody moved for about ten seconds. Finally, the robbers looked at each other and burst out laughing. They dropped their loot and fell to the pavement screaming in hysterics.

Almost immediately, the cops arrived and arrested the crooks.

"Let that be a lesson to you," cried Captain Underpants. "Never underestimate the power of underwear!"

The police chief, looking quite angry, marched over to Captain Underpants.

"And just who the heck are *you* supposed to be?" the police chief demanded.

"Why, *I'm* Captain Underpants, the world's greatest superhero," said Captain Underpants. "I fight for Truth, Justice and *all* that is Pre-Shrunk and Cottony!"

"Oh, *YEAH*!!?" shouted the police chief. "Cuff him, boys!"

One of the cops took out his handcuffs and grabbed Captain Underpants by the arm.

"Uh-oh!" cried George. "We gotta roll!" Together the two boys zoomed into the crowd, weaving in and out of cops and bystanders. Harold skated up to Captain Underpants and knocked the superhero off his feet. George caught him and the boys skated away with Captain Underpants on their shoulders.

"Stop!" cried the cops, but it was too late. George, Harold and Captain Underpants were gone.

CHAPTER 14
THE BIG BANG

After their quick escape, George, Harold, and Captain Underpants stopped on a deserted street corner to catch their breath.

"OK," said George. "Let's de-hypnotize him quick, before something else . . .

. . . happens!"

KA-BOOM

A huge explosion came from the Rare Crystal Shop across the street. Heavy smoke poured out of the building. Suddenly, two robots with one stolen crystal emerged from the smoke and jumped into an old van.

"Did I just see two *ROBOTS* get into a van?" asked Harold.

"You know," said George, "up until *now* this story was almost *believable*!"

"Well, believable or not," said Harold, "we're not getting involved. I repeat: We are *NOT* getting involved!"

Just then, Captain Underpants leaped from the street corner and dashed in front of the van.

"Stop, in the name of underwear!" he cried.

"Uh-oh," said George. "I think we're *involved*."

The two robots started up the van and swerved around Captain Underpants. Unfortunately, the van brushed up against his red cape, and it got caught. With a mighty *jerk*, Captain Underpants flipped backward, and the van pulled him along as it drove away.

"GRAB HIM!" cried George.

The two boys skateboarded with all their might towards the speeding van and grabbed Captain Underpants by the ankles.

"HEEEEEEELLLLLLLP!" they cried as the van pulled them through the city streets.

"Mummy," said a little boy sitting on a bench, "I just saw two robots driving a van with a guy in his underwear hanging off the back by a red cape, pulling two boys on skateboards behind him with his feet."

"How do you expect me to believe such a ridiculous story?" asked his mother.

Finally, the van came to a screeching halt in front of an old abandoned warehouse. The sudden stop made Captain Underpants flip over the roof of the van and crash through the front door of the building.

"Well, well, well," said a strange voice from inside the warehouse. "It looks as if we have a *visitor*."

76

CHAPTER 15
DR NAPPY

George and Harold hid behind the van until the coast was clear. Then they sneaked up to the hole in the door and peeked inside.

Captain Underpants was all tied up, the two robots were standing guard, and a strange little man wearing a nappy was laughing maniacally.

"I am the evil Dr Nappy," the strange little man told Captain Underpants. "And you will be the first to witness my takeover of the *world*!"

Dr Diaper placed the stolen crystal into a large machine called the *Laser-Matic 2000*. The machine started to light up and make loud noises. Heavy gears began shifting and spinning, and a laser beam from the crystal shot straight up through a hole in the roof.

"In exactly twenty minutes, this laser beam will blow up the moon and send huge chunks of it crashing down upon every major city in the world!" laughed Dr Nappy. "Then, I will rise from the rubble and take over the planet!"

"Only one thing can help us now," said George.

"What?" asked Harold.

"Rubber doggy doo-doo," said George.

Harold took the fake doggy doo-doo and a slingshot from George's backpack and handed them to him.

"Be careful," said Harold. "The fate of the entire planet is in your hands!"

With careful and precise aim, George shot the rubber doo-doo through the air and across the room. It landed with a *plop*! – right at the feet of Dr Nappy.

"Yessss!" whispered George and Harold.

Dr Nappy looked down at the doo-doo between his feet and turned bright red.

"Oh, dear me!" he cried. "I'm dreadfully embarrassed! Please excuse me."

He began to waddle towards the toilet. "This has never happened to me before, I assure you," he said. "I-I guess with all the excitement, I just . . . I just. . . Oh, dear! Oh, dear!"

While Dr Nappy was off changing himself, George and Harold sneaked into the old warehouse.

Immediately, the robots detected the boys and began marching toward them. "Destroy the intruders!" said the robots. "Destroy the intruders!"

George and Harold screamed and ran to the back of the warehouse. Luckily, George found two old boards and gave one of them to Harold.

"We're not going to have to resort to extremely graphic violence, are we?" asked Harold.

"I sure hope not," said George.

CHAPTER 16
THE EXTREMELY GRAPHIC VIOLENCE CHAPTER

WARNING:

The following chapter contains graphic scenes showing two boys beating the tar out of a couple of robots.

If you have high blood pressure, or if you faint at the sight of motor oil, we strongly urge you to take better care of yourself and stop being such a baby.

Introducing
FLIP-O
As everybody knows, nothing enhances silly action sequences more than cheesy animation.
And so, for the first time inthe history of great literature, we proudly bring you the latest in cheesy animation technology: The art of Flip-O-Rama.

O·RAMA

HERE'S HOW IT WORKS!

Step 1
Place your *left* hand inside the dotted lines marked "LEFT HAND HERE." Hold the book open *flat*.

Step 2
Grasp the *right-hand* page with your right thumb and index finger (inside the dotted lines marked "RIGHT THUMB HERE")

Step 3
Now *quickly* flip the right-hand page back and forth until the picture appears to be *animated*.

(For extra fun, try adding your own sound-effects!)

FLIP-O-RAMA 1

(pages 87 and 89)

Remember, flip *only* page 87.
While you are flipping, be sure you
can see the picture on page 87
and the one on page 89.
If you flip quickly, the two
pictures will start to look like
<u>one</u> *animated* picture.

Don't forget to
add your own sound-effects!

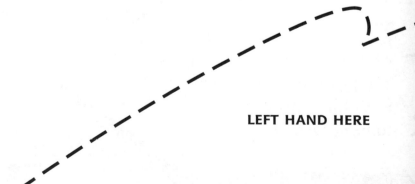

LEFT HAND HERE

ROBOT RAMPAGE!

ROBOT RAMPAGE!

FLIP-O-RAMA 2

(pages 91 and 93)

Remember, flip *only* page 91.
While you are flipping, be sure you
can see the picture on page 91
and the one on page 93.
If you flip quickly, the two
pictures will start to look like
<u>one</u> *animated* picture.

Don't forget to
add your own sound-effects!

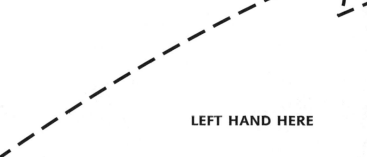

LEFT HAND HERE

GEORGE SAVES HAROLD!

RIGHT THUMB HERE

RIGHT
INDEX
FINGER
HERE

GEORGE SAVES HAROLD!

FLIP-O-RAMA 3

(pages 95 and 97)

Remember, flip *only* page 95.
While you are flipping, be sure you
can see the picture on page 95
and the one on page 97.
If you flip quickly, the two
pictures will start to look like
<u>one</u> *animated* picture.

Don't forget to
add your own sound-effects!

LEFT HAND HERE

HAROLD RETURNS
THE FAVOUR!

RIGHT
THUMB
HERE

RIGHT
INDEX
FINGER
HERE

HAROLD RETURNS
THE FAVOUR!

FLIP-O-RAMA 4

(pages 99 and 101)

Remember, flip *only* page 99.
While you are flipping, be sure you
can see the picture on page 99
and the one on page 101.
If you flip quickly, the two
pictures will start to look like
<u>one</u> *animated* picture.

Don't forget to
add your own sound-effects!

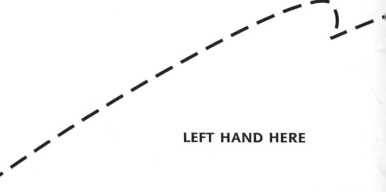

LEFT HAND HERE

MIXED NUTS
(...AND BOLTS!)

RIGHT
THUMB
HERE

MIXED NUTS
(...AND BOLTS!)

CHAPTER 17
THE ESCAPE

After defeating the robots, George and Harold untied Captain Underpants.

"Come on!" cried Harold. "Let's get out of here!"

"Wait!" said Captain Underpants. "We have to save the world first!"

So George, Harold and Captain Underpants frantically looked all over the *Laser-Matic 2000*, searching for a way to shut it down and stop the inevitable disaster.

"Ummm," said Harold. "I think *this* might be the lever we want."

He pulled the "Self-Destruct" lever with all his might. Suddenly, the *Laser-Matic 2000* began to sputter and shake. The huge laser beam turned off, and pieces of the machine began flying off in all directions.

"It's gonna BLOW!" cried Harold. "RUN FOR YOUR LIVES!"

SELF-
DESTRUCT
(PLEASE
DON'T PULL)

TIC
00

"*NOT SO FAST!*" screamed Dr Nappy, who had appeared out of nowhere. "You demolished my robots. You *destroyed* my *Laser-Matic 2000*. And you ruined my one chance to take over the world – but you won't live to tell the tale!" Dr Nappy pulled out his *Nappy-Matic 2000* ray gun, and pointed it at George, Harold and Captain Underpants.

Captain Underpants quickly stretched a pair of
underwear and shot it at Dr Nappy. The underwear
landed right on the evil doctor's head.
"Help!" cried Dr Nappy. "I can't see! I can't see!"

George and Harold ran out of the warehouse as fast as they could.

"Great shot, Captain Underpants!" cried Harold.

"There's just one thing I don't understand," said George. "Where'd you get the *extra* pair of underwear?"

"What extra pair?" said Captain Underpants.

"Never mind that," cried George, "let's just get out of here before that *Laser-Matic 2000* thing ex . . .

. . . plodes!"

The *Laser-Matic 2000* blew up, tearing apart the old warehouse. It sent flaming shards of red-hot metal in every direction. Fire fell from the skies around our heroes, and the earth began to crumble beneath their feet.

"Oh, NO!" cried Harold. *"WE'RE DOOMED!"*

CHAPTER 18
TO MAKE A LONG STORY SHORT

They got away.

CHAPTER 19
BACK TO SCHOOL

George, Harold and Captain Underpants made a quick stop outside the police station. They tied Dr Nappy to a lamppost and attached a note to him.

"There!" said Captain Underpants. "That ought to explain everything."

Then George and Harold led Captain Underpants back to Jerome Horwitz Elementary School.

"Why are we going *here*?" asked Captain Underpants.

"Well," said George, "you have to do some *undercover* work."

"Yeah," said Harold, reaching into his backpack. "Put these clothes on, and make it snappy!"

"Don't forget your hair," said George.

Captain Underpants quickly got dressed behind some bushes. "Well, how do I look?" he asked.

"Pretty good," said George. "Now try to look really angry!"

Captain Underpants made the nastiest face he could.

"You know," said Harold, "he kinda looks like Mr Krupp!"

"*Harold,*" whispered George, "he is Mr Krupp!"

"Oh, yeah," said Harold. "I almost forgot."

Before long, they were all back inside Mr Krupp's office.

"OK, Captain Underpants," said George, "you are now Mr Krupp."

"Snap your fingers," whispered Harold.

"Oh, yeah," said George. *Snap!* "You are now Mr Krupp."

"Who's Mr Krupp?" asked Captain Underpants.

"Oh, NO!" cried Harold. *"It's not working!"*

The boys tried again and again to de-hypnotize Captain Underpants, but *nothing* seemed to work.

116

"Hmmm," said Harold. "Let me see the instruction manual for that ring."

George checked his trouser pocket.

"Umm," said George, "I think I *lost* it."

"You WHAT?" cried Harold. The two boys searched frantically through the office, but the 3-D Hypno-Ring instruction manual was nowhere to be found.

"Never mind," said George. "I have an idea." He removed the flowers from a large vase in the corner. Then he poured out all of the water over Captain Underpants' head.

"What did you do *that* for?" cried Harold.

"I saw 'em do this in a cartoon once," said George, "so it's *gotta* work!"

After a few minutes, Mr Krupp slowly came to. "What's going on here?" he demanded. "And why am I all wet!!?"

George and Harold had never been so glad to see Mr Krupp in all their lives.

"I'm so happy I could cry," said Harold.

"Well, you're *gonna* cry when I give that videotape to the football team!" shouted Mr Krupp. "I've *had it* with you two!"

Principal Krupp took the videotape out of his
filing cabinet. "You boys are *dead meat*!" he sneered.
He stormed out of his office with the video and headed
towards the gym.

George and Harold smiled. "Wait till the football team
sees *that* video!" said Harold.

"Yeah," said George, "I sure hope they like singing
purple dragons!"

"Hey, look," said George. "I found the 3-D Hypno-Ring instruction manual. It was in my *shirt* pocket, not my trouser pocket!"

"Well, throw that thing away," said Harold. "We'll never need it again."

"I certainly hope not," said George.

WARNING!!!

Whatever you do, don't put water on anybody's head when they are in a trance! This will cause the hypnotized person to slip back and forth from trance to reality whenever they hear the sound of fingers snapping.

TRASH

CHAPTER 20
THE END?

LA-LA-LA-LA- WE LOVE BOOMER - LA-LA

PURPLE DRAGON SING-A-LONG FRIENDS

PURPLE DRAGON SING-A-LONG FRIENDS

PURPLE DRAGON SING-A-LONG FRIENDS

   Things at Jerome Horwitz Elementary School were never quite the same after that fateful day.
   The football team enjoyed Mr Krupp's video so much that they changed their name from the Knuckleheads to the Purple Dragon Sing-A-Long Friends. The name change didn't go down too well with the fans, but hey, who's going to argue with a bunch of linebackers?
   George and Harold went back to their old

121

ways, pulling pranks, cracking jokes and making new comic books.

They had to keep an eye on Mr Krupp, though . . .

. . . because for some *strange* reason, every time he heard the sound of fingers snapping . . .

Snap!

. . . Principal Krupp turned *back* into . . .

. . . you know who!

"Oh, no!" cried Harold.
"Here we go *again*!" said George.

FOR KATHY AND ANAMIKA

George and Harold's College O' Art

PAY ATTENTION NOW--- This will be on The Test!

Hi everybody. It's Time To LEARN How To make Your Own comic Books!

It's EASY--- And FUN!!!

ALL You NEED is some PAPER, Pencils, ERASERS AND A STAPLER.

ERASER

MR. STAPLEY

FiRST You HAVE To Think up A STORY.

And The best WAY To do THAT is To CREATE CHARACTERS.

MANY COMIC BOOKS END WITH A BIG FIGHT. IF YOU HAVE TROUBLE WRITING ACTION SCENES, YOU CAN ALWAYS USE FLIP-O-RAMA INSTEAD.

TURN TO PAGE 150 TO LEARN HOW TO MAKE YOUR VERY OWN FLIP-O-RAMAS.

WHEN YOU'RE FINALLY DONE, MAKE A COVER. THEN STAPLE ALL OF YOUR PAGES TOGETHER.

TA-DAAA! YOUR VERY OWN COMIC BOOK!

NOW GO MAKE COPIES OF IT AND SELL THEM IN THE PLAYGROUND !!!

(ANSWER ON PAGE 219)

HOW TO DRAW CAPTAIN UNDERPANTS

1.

2.

3.

4.

5.

6.

7.

8.

9.

10.

11.

12.

13.

14.

15.

16.

(ANSWER ON PAGE 219)

140

When your victim leans back to put the penny on his chin...

...pour your water into the funnel.

...now RUN!

HA·HA·HA A·HA·HA·HA!

THE PERILOUS PUZZLE OF PROFESSOR POOPYPANTS

Across
2. The alien spacemen were named Zorx, Klax, and _____.
4. Harold's best friend is _____.
5. "George is the kid on the left with the _____ and the flat-top."
7. George's best friend is _____.
8. Don't get "weeded out" by the Deliriously Dangerous Death-Defying _____ of Doom.
10. Dr Nappy wanted to blow up the _____.
12. Captain Underpants is also known as a principal named Mr _____.
14. Don't get flushed by the Turbo _____ 2000!
15. "Yum, _____, eat 'em up!"

Down
1. "Never underestimate the power of _____."
3. _____ Horwitz Elementary School
4. Don't get blown up by the Goosy-_____ 4000.
6. Ms Ribble is George and Harold's _____.
7. "Harold is the one on the right with the T-shirt and the bad _____."

9. Captain Underpants fights crime with Wedgie _____.

11. Professor Poopypants's first name.

13. Don't get shrunk by the Shrinky-_____ 2000.

(ANSWERS ON PAGE 220)

145

HOW TO DRAW
THE TURBO TOILET 2000

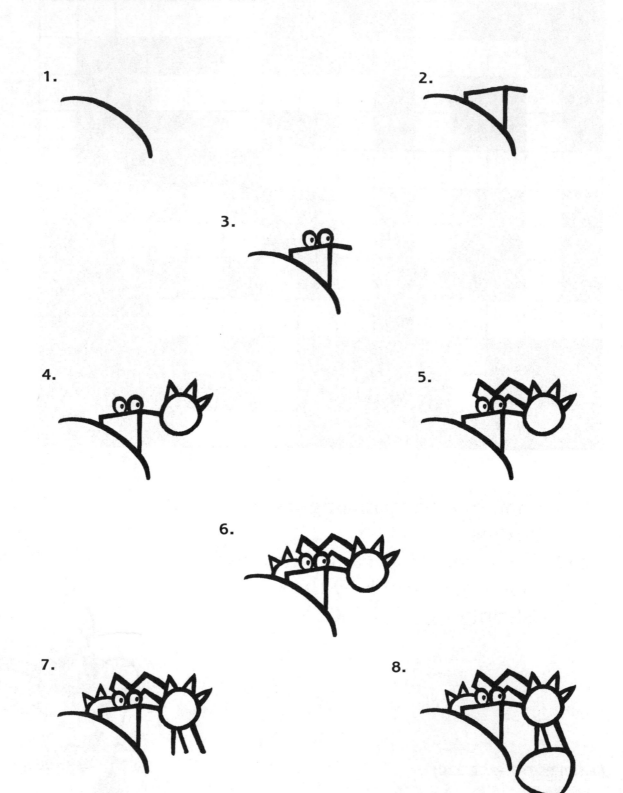

1.

2.

3.

4.

5.

6.

7.

8.

9.

10.

11.

12.

13.

14.

15.

16.

```
C H I C K E N O D I C D
B J B U B B L E T O F U
D R A Z Z I G K O N D Q
L G E X N O I T C C R B
A I D T R M I O I U R I
N G Z I S E A V P D H E
A G L A A M K P T A I C
N L G G R P A N O O N T
A E I I E D E H I T O L
B U R G E R D R L T T O
K J D F R A B O E V S Y
G E L K C I P I T V V R
G Y E K N O M R L U I X
W A F F L E P I Z Z A L
```

(ANSWER ON PAGE 220)

BECAUSE MOST PAPER IS A LITTLE TRANSPARENT, YOU SHOULD STILL KINDA BE ABLE TO SEE YOUR DRAWING UNDERNEATH.

I CAN KINDA SEE IT!

IF YOU CAN'T SEE YOUR DRAWING UNDERNEATH THE TOP SHEET OF PAPER, JUST HOLD IT UP TO A SUNNY WINDOW.

COOL!

NOW WE'RE GOING TO DO SOME TRACING ON THE TOP PAGE. THE 1ST RULE IS: IF YOU DON'T WANT SOMETHING TO MOVE, TRACE IT!!!

153

154

And since he's dribbling the ball on the floor, I'll re-draw the ball down on the floor.

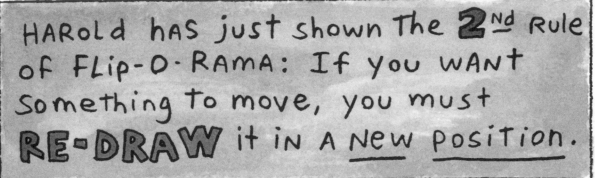

HAROLD has just shown The **2**<u>ND</u> Rule of FLip-O-RAmA: If you WANT Something to move, you must **RE-DRAW** it in A <u>NEW</u> <u>position</u>.

⭐ Look at HAROLD'S Two dRAWINGS BeLow... Notice the differences.

FIRST dRAWING (Bottom page)

Second dRAWING (TOP PAGE)

NOTE: When flipping your home-made FLIP-O-RAMAS, ONLY FLIP The Top Page. ALSO, MAKE SURE That you CAN see both pictures AS you FLIP.

Top page Flips up and down.

BOTTOM PAGE STAYS FLAT.

Hold here.

158

Left hand Here.

Right thume Here

★ ★ ★ ★ ★ ★ SPESHEL NOTES
FOR FLIP-O-RAMISTS

1. Typing paper and notebook paper work best.

2. Although you need to trace, don't use tracing paper. It will ruin the Affect.

3. Grown-ups will freak out if your flip-o-Ramas Feacher "people" beating each other up. To get around this, draw robots and monsters instead. (For some REASon, Grown-ups think thats O.K. ...Go Figure!)

4. You can get good ideas by studying the FLIP-O-RamAS in The "CAptain Underpants" and "Ricky Ricotta" Books.

LAFFS

"Knock knock?"

"Who's there?"

"I'm a pile-up."

"I'm a pile-up who?"

"No, you're not! Don't be so hard on yourself, buddy!"

Q) What did the mummy buffalo say to the baby buffalo when he went off to school?

A) Bison.

Q) What does lightning wear beneath its clothes?

A) Thunderwear.

Q) What should you do if you get swallowed by an elephant?

A) Jump up and down until you're all pooped out.

Q) Why did batman cross his legs?

A) He had to go to the bat-room.

Q) If you had fifty bananas in one hand, and twenty-five litres of ice-cream in the other, what would you have?

A) Really big hands.

163

HOW TO DRAW
PROFESSOR POOPYPANTS

11.

12.

13.

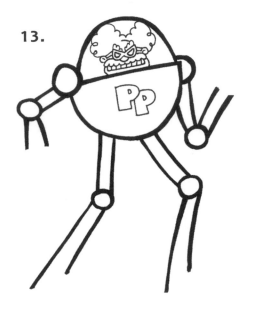

14.

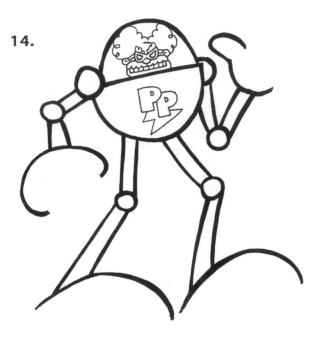

15.

16.

THE CAFETERIA LADIES' CRAZY CROSSWORD

Across

3. Dr _____ was defeated soon after George shot fake doggy doo-doo at him.
5. *The Attack of the* _____ *Toilets*.
6. Watch out for the Equally Evil Lunchroom _____ Nerds.
8. Pippy P. Poopypants invented the _____ Jogger 2000.
10. "Hooray for Captain _____!"
11. Don't drink the Evil Zombie Nerd _____!
13. Captain Underpants often shouts "_____-La-Laaaaa!"
14. *Cheesy Animation Technology* is more commonly known as _____-O-Rama.

Down

1. *The Adventures of _____ Underpants.*
2. Mr Krupp was transformed into a superhero by the 3-D Hypno-_____.
4. *The Perilous Plot of ____ Poopypants.*
7. Zorx, Klax and Jennifer were evil guys from outer _____.
9. A popular way to misspell the word "laughs".
12. Captain Underpants wears a red _____.

(ANSWERS ON PAGE 220)

H S T I U C S I B G H
U P E S K N U H C E T
M I R L I O Y U A H U
P L J A K P E D S O M
E V R Q O N N N J H O
R B V S Q U I R T O Q
D Q M W S F H R Q R F
I H A G F A N E P T Q
N B R E A T H I F S P
C M R E K N O H A R F
K S S F S O J S T T N
J P A N T S U U T G B
J C L O U E I T Y B U
E D Y E S B C K D W T
Q U E F H S E O T V T

(ANSWERS ON PAGE 221)

169

WELCOME TO A BRAND-NEW CAPTAIN UNDERPANTS STORY. . . AND YOU'RE THE STAR!

Before you read the story on the following pages, go through and find all the blanks. Below each blank is a small description of what you need to write in the blank. Just fill in the blank with an appropriate word.

For example, if the blank looks like this:

_____, you would think up an adjective
(an adjective)

and put it in the blank like this: _____stinky_____.
(an adjective)

Remember, don't read the story first. It's more fun if you go through and fill in the blanks first, THEN read the story.

When you're done, follow the instructions at the bottom of each page to complete the illustrations. Cool, huh?

JUST FOR REMINDERS:
a **Verb** is an <u>action</u> word (like jump, swim, kick, squish, run, etc.)
an **Adjective** is a word that <u>describes</u> a person, place
or thing (lumpy, dumb, purple, hairy, etc.)

CAPTAIN UNDERPANTS VS THE EVIL MONSTER

(STARRING GEORGE, HAROLD AND YOU!)

Once upon a time, George, Harold and their friend,

___Ryan___, were busy studying about the
(your name)

wonders of ___Stinky___ ___Slime___,
(an adjective)   (disgusting things)

when their new science teacher, Mr ___Prickles___,
(a funny name)

accidentally spilled some ___Bogies___
(a gross adjective)

___goo___ on a pile of toxic ___Pigs___.
(a liquid)   (silly things)

(Draw yourself
sitting here)

(Draw the teacher spilling
liquid on to some toxic stuff)

Suddenly, the pile began to morph into

a giant, evil ___Shoe___ .

"Help," cried ___Jessrey___ , "a

giant, evil ___Shoe___

just stepped on my lunchbox and ate up

___Mr Statsy___ !"

"Oh NO!" cried Mr Krupp. "The poor

lunchbox!"

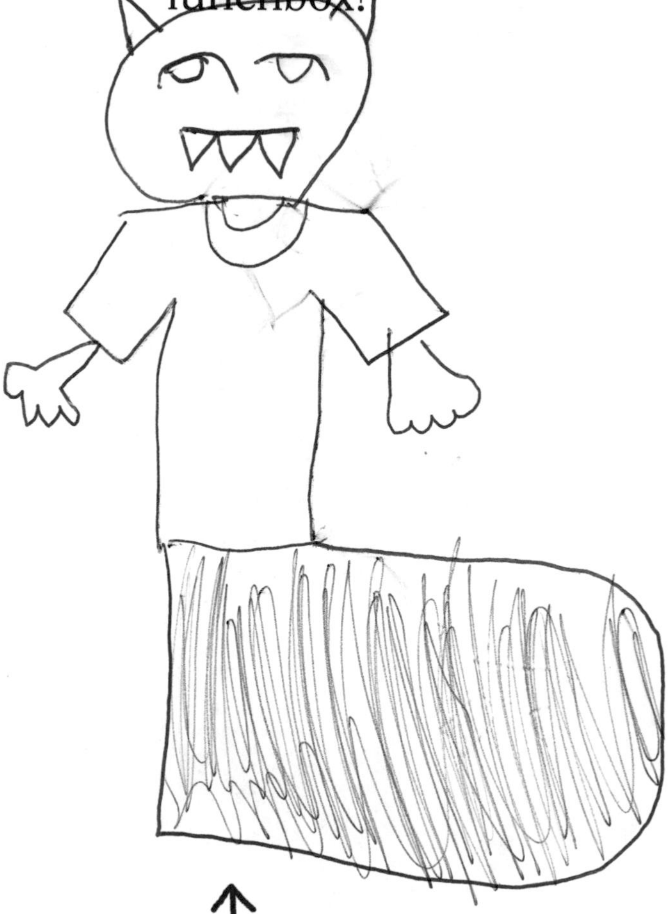

(Draw the giant,
evil monster)

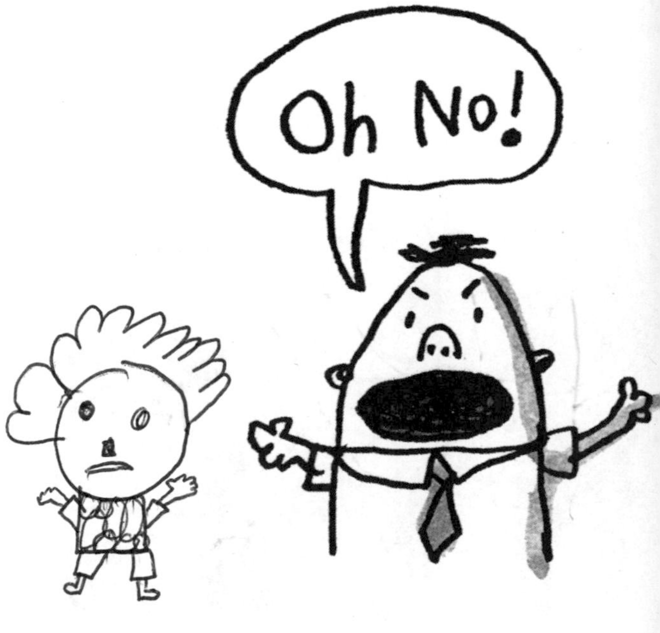

Oh No!

(Draw the kid in
your class)

George, Harold and _____Ryan_____ tried to

escape by hiding behind a _____cuBoard_____ .

(your name)

Then _____Ryan_____ snapped _____His_____

(a very small thing)

(your name)   (either "his" or "her")

fingers.

Soon, a _____Smiley_____ grin came across

(an adjective)

Mr Krupp's face as he dropped _a_ _Key_

(an adjective)

his _____Pants_____ and ran to his office.

(an article of clothing)

↑   ↑

(Draw yourself)   (Draw the thing you're all   (Draw the giant,
                     hiding behind)   evil monster)

173

Soon, Captain Underpants __5mashed__

through the wall. He grabbed a __rock__

__Pants__ and hit the monster on its

__head__ .

"Ouchies!" screamed the monster. It turned and

_____ Captain Underpants on his

_____ .

(Draw
yourself)

(Draw the monster fighting
Captain Underpants)

_____ quickly mixed up a bottle of
(your name)

_____ with a jar of toxic,
(something a kid would drink)

_____ _____ .
(an adjective)   (disgusting things)

"Hey, _____ ," said George, "where'd
(your name)

you find that jar of crazy stuff?!!?"

"It was right here next to this barrel of toxic

_____ _____," said
(an adjective)   (different disgusting things)

_____ .
(your name)

"Oh," said Harold. "That makes sense."

_____
↑
(Draw yourself creating
a strange mixture)

↑
(Draw the contents of the barrel
coming out the top)

_____ shook up the strange mixture and
(your name)

threw it at the monster.

" _____!" screamed the monster as
(something you might scream or cheer)

it fell over and died of a massive _____ attack.
(a body part)

"That makes sense, too," said George.

Unfortunately, some of the mixture splashed on

Captain Underpants's head, and he turned back into

Mr Krupp.

↑

(Draw yourself throwing the strange
concoction on to the monster)

(Draw the monster
getting splashed)

"HOLY _____ _____ !"
(an adjective)   (silly animals)

shouted Mr Krupp. "I'll bet that George, Harold and

_____ are responsible for this mess!" So he
(your name)

punished the three kids by making them _____
(an action verb)

in the _____ for _____ hours.
(a room in the school)   (a number)

"This has got to be the dumbest story we've ever been

in," said George.

"Don't blame me," said Harold. "_____
(your name)

wrote it!"

↑

(Draw yourself
looking guilty)

ZORX, KLAX AND Jennifer's Big, BAD BATCH of ZOMBIE NERD Juice

(ANSWER ON PAGE 221)

178

FINAL EXAM

Hi everybody!
One thing I know for sure is that kids LOVE to study and take tests! That's why we've included this incredibly difficult FINAL EXAM! Make sure you've studied BOTH of George and Harold's College o' Art comics. When you think you're ready, take out a pencil, turn the page and begin. Good luck!

1. What's the BEST way to think up a story?

a) create characters

b) put a grilled cheese sandwich on your head

c) roll around in steak sauce, then bark like a dog

2. What is often to blame for creating monsters?

a) society

b) school dinners

c) nuclear waste

3. What two things also help you think up stories?

a) brainstorming and day dreaming

b) braindreaming and daystorming

c) daybraining and dreamstorming

4. Don't worry about making mistakes. That's why they invented ____.

a) lawyers

b) erasers

c) soap-on-a-rope

5. If you have trouble writing action scenes, you can always use ___.

a) a ghost writer

b) Flip-O-Rama

c) egg salad

6. When making comics, be prepared to:

a) win friends and influence people

b) smell like cheese puffs

c) suffer for your art

7. What's the world's EASIEST Flip-O-Rama?

a) a guy with a chicken up his nose

b) a guy with a basketball

c) a guy with a basketball up his nose

8. The FIRST rule of Flip-O-Rama is: If you don't want something to move, _____.

a) trace it

b) put it in a "time-out"

c) threaten to stop the car

9. The SECOND rule of Flip-O-Rama is: If you want something to move, you must _____.

a) make rude noises with your armpits

b) drink lots of prune juice

c) re-draw it in a new position

10. The more you practise, _____.

a) the better you get

b) the dumber you get

c) the stinkier you get

Now put your pencil down, and let's see how you did.

ANSWERS:
1: a, 2: c (though technically "b" is also correct),
3: a, 4: b, 5: b, 6: c, 7: b, 8: a, 9: c, 10: a

If you got at least 6 right, CONGRATULATIONS! You've just graduated from George and Harold's College o' Art.

Q) Why do sharks live in salt water?

A) Because pepper water makes them sneeze.

Q) How do you make a tissue dance?

A) Put a little boogie into it.

Q) Why did Tigger stick his head in the toilet?

A) He was looking for "Pooh".

Q) Who is Peter Pan's worst-smelling friend?

A) Stinkerbell.

Q) What nationality are you when you go to the bathroom?

A) European.

A woman walks into a pet store and says, "Can I get a puppy for my daughter?" "Sorry, lady," says the pet store owner. "We don't do swaps."

Hairy Potty shot his lazer and made a hole in the wall.

ZAP

I'm free!!!

Then he ran around causing mischiff.

BOB'S DINER
AT BOB'S DINER, you'll find that we pick the best ingredyents. Your nose KNOWS the difrense!

Hmmm.

ZAP

BOB'S
AT BOB'S DINER, we pick your nose

HAW HAW HAW

Then Hairy Potty ran to a school.

LA-LA LA-LA

FLIP-O-RAMA # 1

(pages 197 and 199)

Remember, flip only page 197 while you are fliping, be sure you can see the pitcher on page 197 And the one on Page 199.

If you flip Quickly, the two pitchers will start to Look Like One Animated pitcher.

Left Hand Here

The EyeBall Basher

Right thume Here

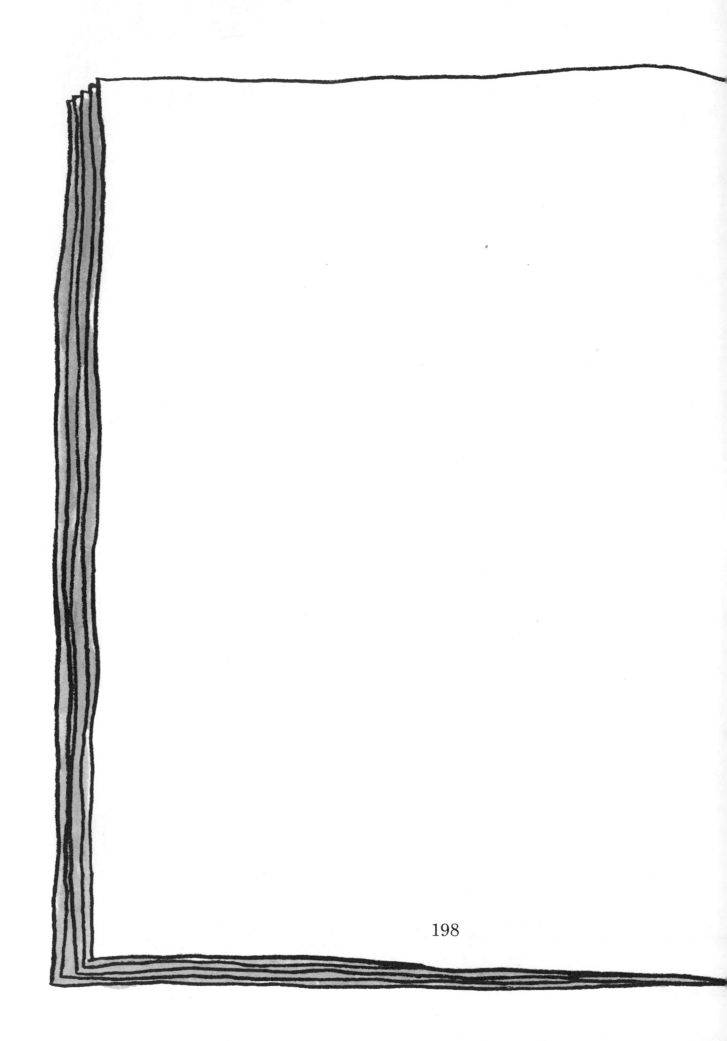

198

The EyeBall Basher

FLIP-O-RAMA #2

(pages 201 And 203)

Remember, flip only page 201 while you are fliping, be sure you can see the pitcher on page 201 And the one on page 203.

If you flip quickly, the two pitchers will start to look like one Animated pitcher.

Left Hand Here

THE KOO-KOO CLAP

201

right thume Here

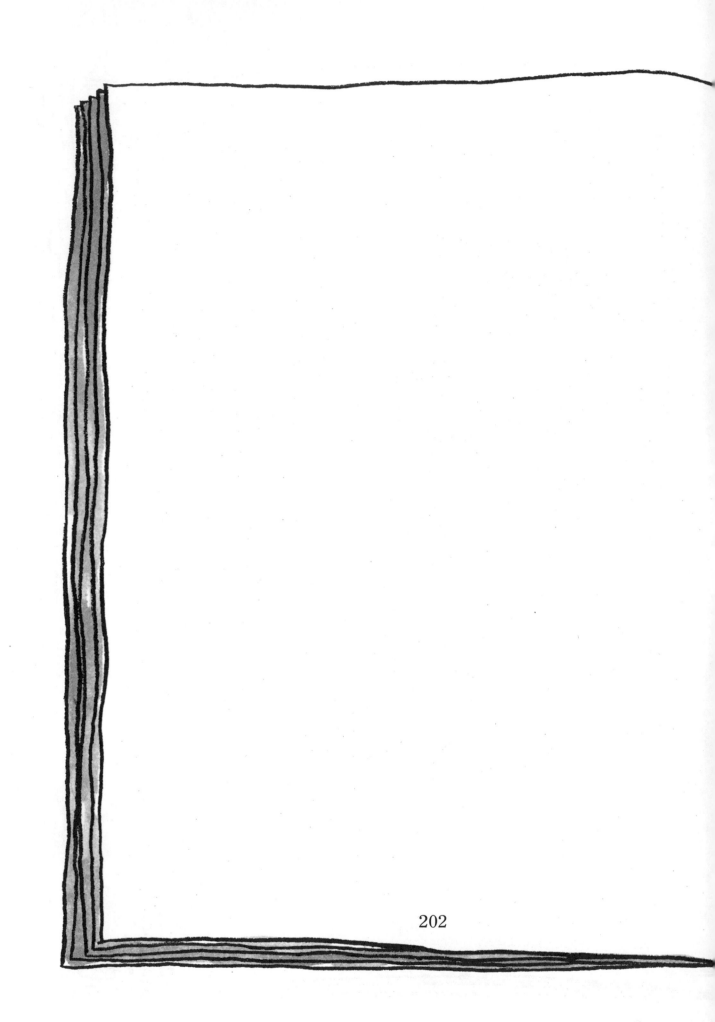

THE KOO-KOO CLAP

FLIP·O·RAMA #3

(pages 205 and 207)

Remember, flip <u>only</u> page 205 while you are fliping, be sure you can see the pitcher on page 205 <u>And</u> the one on page 207.

If you flip Quickly, the two pitchers will start to look like <u>One</u> Animated pitcher.

Left Hand Here

The Potty Pounder

Right
Thume
Here

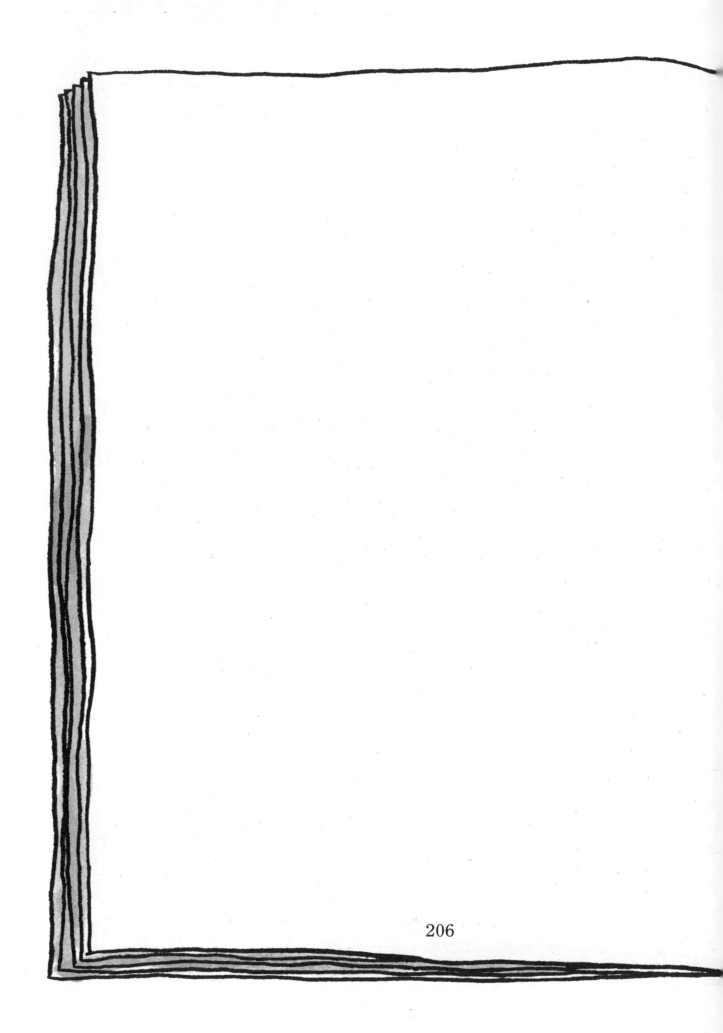

The Potty Pounder

FLIP·O·RAMA # 4

(pages 209 and 211)

Remember, flip only page 209 while you are fliping, be sure you can see the pitcher on page 209 And the one on page 211.

If you flip Quickly, the two pitchers will start to look like One Animated pitcher.

Left Hand Here

The Psycko Stomp

Right Thume Here

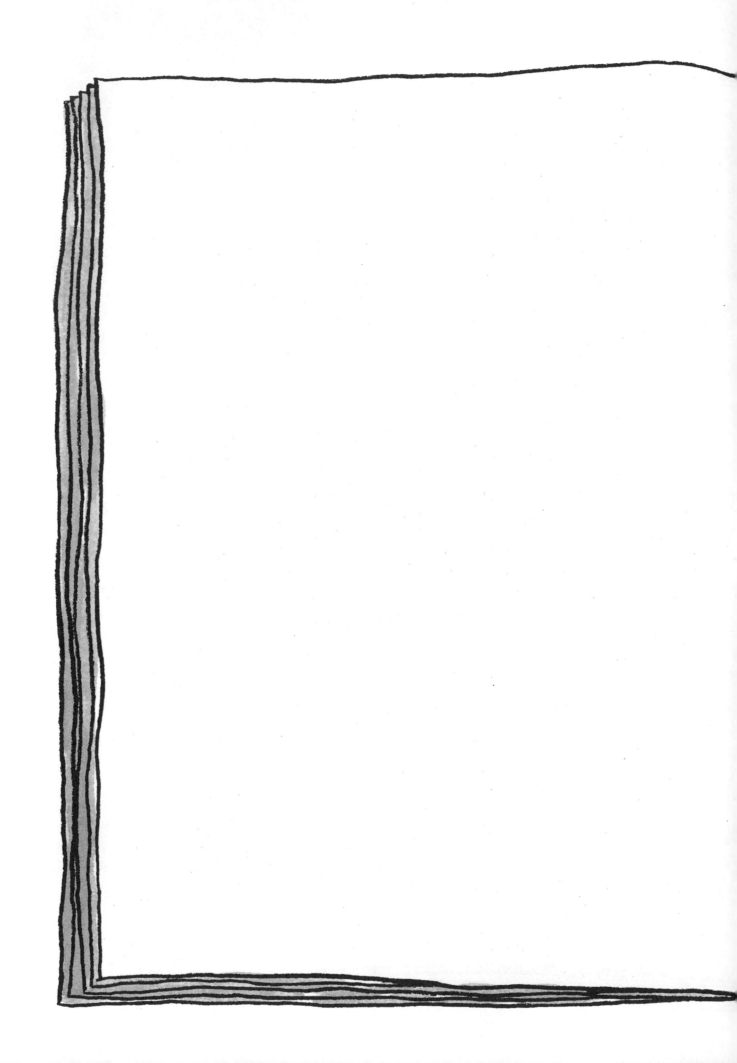

The Psycko Stomp

ANSWERS

WORD SEARCH P. 137

MAZE P. 140

**CROSSWORD
P. 145**

**WORD SEARCH
P. 149**

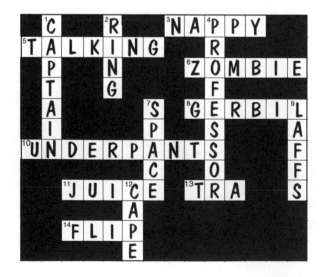

**CROSSWORD
P. 167**

WORD SEARCH
P. 169

H	S	T	I	U	C	S	I	B	G	H
U	P	E	S	K	N	U	H	C	E	T
M	I	L	R	L	I	O	Y	U	A	U
P	L	V	J	A	K	P	E	D	S	O
E	V	R	Q	O	N	N	N	J	H	M
R	B	B	V	S	Q	U	I	R	T	Q
D	Q	M	W	S	F	H	R	Q	R	F
I	H	H	A	G	F	A	N	E	T	Q
N	B	R	E	A	T	H	I	F	S	F
C	M	R	E	K	N	O	H	A	R	F
K	S	S	F	S	O	J	S	T	R	N
J	P	A	N	T	S	U	U	T	G	B
J	C	L	O	U	E	I	T	Y	B	U
E	D	Y	E	S	B	C	K	D	W	T
Q	U	E	F	H	S	E	O	T	V	T

MAZE
P. 178

221

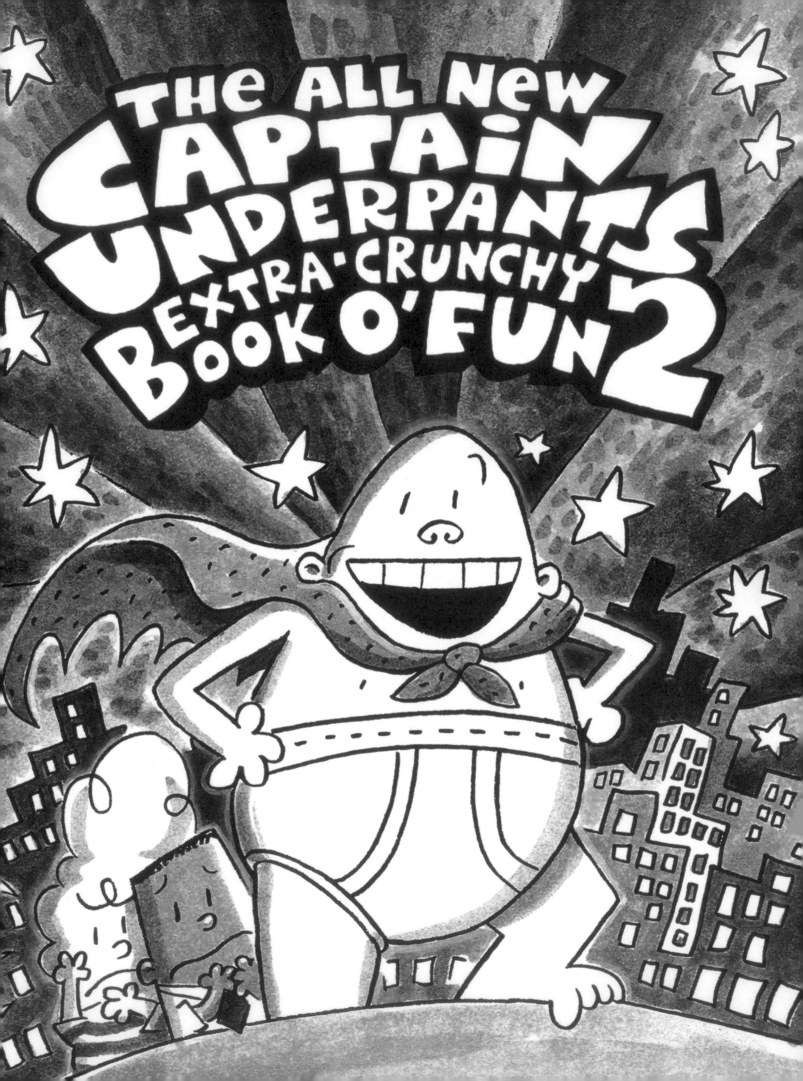

FOR ELIZABETH AND RACHEL

WEDGIE-POWERED WORD FIND

Try to find the names below in the puzzle on the right.
Look up, down, backwards and diagonally.

CHARACTER NAME BONUS QUIZ:

How well do you know your UNDERPANTS?
Draw lines from the first names in Chart A
to the matching last names in Chart B.

CHART A	Chart B
Benny	Beard
Billy	Fyde
George	Hoskins
Harold	Hutchins
Melvin	Krupp
Morty	Poopypants
Pippy	Ribble
Tara	Sneedly
Tippy	Tinkletrousers

S T N A P Y P O O P
R U O R L Y H Q N A
E G N L V X T V F F
S N I H C T U H L Z
U B V M A L O E S A
O A L F O S G D R J
R U E C K R R A Q E
T F M I O A T D D I
E S N E E D L Y V E
L S G B L O F L R S
K Q F F R B P C P U
N S E A E R B I C R
I A H N Y P P I T Z
T X N M J P P U R K
K Y Q B Y R Z X D C

(ANSWER ON PAGE 317)

HOW TO DRAW
CAPTAIN UNDERPANTS

1.

2.

3.

4.

5.

6.

7.

8.

9.

10.

11.

12.

13.

14.

15.

16.

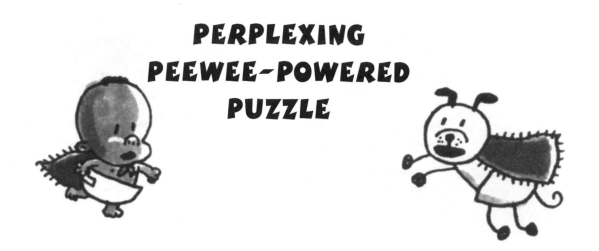

PERPLEXING PEEWEE-POWERED PUZZLE

Across

3. Captain Underpants fights for Truth, Justice, and all that is Pre-Shrunk and _____!

5. A flushable porcelain bowl.

7. "Tra-_____-Laaaaa!"

8. Super Diaper Baby's archenemy is _____ Doo-Doo.

9. Captain Underpants is nicknamed the _____ Warrior.

10. Super Diaper Baby's best friend is Diaper _____.

11. The only five-letter word (starting with an "s") to appear twice in the last six clues.

14. Watch out for the Wicked Wedgie _____!

15. Liquid spray _____ is the enemy of underwear.

Down

1. The three evil space guys were named _____, Klax, and Jennifer.

2. New Swissland's most famous scientist is Professor _____.

3. Three cheers for _____ Underpants!

4. The Bride of _____ Potty.

6. Beware of the _____-Toilet 2000!

10. Billy Hoskins is better known as Super _____ Baby.

12. Don't spill the Extra-Strength Super _____ Juice!

13. Ms _____ turned into the Wicked Wedgie Woman.

(ANSWER ON PAGE 317)

HOW TO DRAW
MR KRUPP

1.

2.

3.
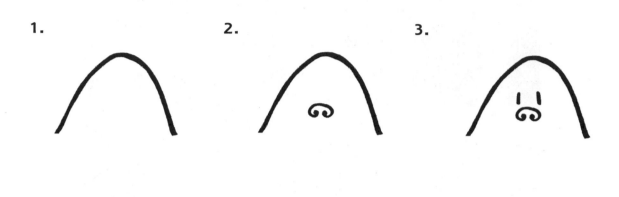

4.

5.

6.

7.

8.

9.

10.

11.

12.

13.

14.

15.

16.

(ANSWER ON PAGE 318)

Q) Why did the cookie cry?

A) Because his mum had been a wafer so long.

"Knock knock."

"Who's there?"

"Olive Toop."

"Olive Toop who?"

"Well so do I, but you don't hear *me* braggin' about it!"

Ms Ribble: Harold, if I gave you two goldfish, and Melvin gave you four goldfish, how many would you have?

Harold: Eleven.

Ms Ribble: *ELEVEN*?!!? Hah! You're *WRONG*, bub!

Harold: No, *you're* wrong. I already have five goldfish back at home!

George: Excuse me, mister, I'd like to buy some toilet paper.

Grocery store clerk: What colour would you like?

George: Just give me white. I'll colour it myself!

Q) What do you get when you cross a porcupine with a great white shark?

A) As far away as possible.

HOW TO DRAW GEORGE

1.

2.

3.

4.

5.

6.

7.

8.

9.

10.

238

11.

12.

13.

14.

15.

16.

HOW TO DRAW HAROLD

1.

2.

3.

4.

5.

6.

7.

8.

9.

10.

240

11.

12.

13.

14.

15.

16.

NOW YOU CAN BE THE STAR
OF YOUR OWN SUPER-CHEESY
CAPTAIN UNDERPANTS STORY!

Before you read the story on the following pages, go through and find all the blanks. Below each blank is a small description of what you need to write in the blank. Just fill in the blank with an appropriate word.

For example, if the blank looks like this:

_____, you would think up an adjective
(an adjective)

and put it in the blank like this:___**snotty**_____ .
(an adjective)

Remember, don't read the story first. It's more fun if you go through and fill in the blanks first, THEN read the story.

When you're done, follow the instructions at the bottom of each page to complete the illustrations. Cool, huh?

> **JUST FOR REMINDERS:**
> a **Verb** is an action word (like jump, swim, kick, squish, run, etc.)
> an **Adjective** is a word that describes a person, place or thing (lumpy, dumb, purple, hairy, etc.)

THE INCREDIBLY STUPID ADVENTURE OF
CAPTAIN UNDERPANTS

This is George Beard, Harold Hutchins and

_____   _____ .
(your first name)   (your last name)

George is the one on the left with the tie and the flat-top.

Harold is the one on the right with the T-shirt and the

bad haircut. _____ is the one in the
              (your first name)

middle with the _____
                    (an adjective)

_____ and the _____
(an article of clothing)   (an adjective)

_____ . Remember that now.
(body part or parts)

(Draw yourself here)

One day, George, Harold and _____
(your first name)

were at school when suddenly, an evil _____
(an adjective)

villain _____ through the door and
(a verb ending in "ed")

roared like a ferocious _____ .
(a harmless insect)

"My name is Commander _____
(a gross adjective)

_____ !" shouted the villain. "And I've come
(a gross thing)

to destroy all the _____ in the world!"
(smelly things)

Commander _____ _____
(the gross adjective and thing you used above)

grabbed a _____ and started hitting
(a piece of furniture)

_____ on the _____with it.
(your PE teacher's name)   (a body part)

"Oh no!" cried _____ . "That villain is
(your first name)

going to hurt the poor _____ !"
(the piece of furniture you used above)

(Draw yourself here)   (Draw your evil villain here)

"We've got to stop that monster!" cried George. He reached into his _____, grabbed a/an
(an article of clothing)

_____ _____, and threw it at the
(an adjective)   (something big)

villain.

Harold found a/an _____ in his
(something bigger)

_____, so he threw that, too. Finally,
(an article of clothing)

_____ reached into his/her _____,
(your name)   (an article of clothing)

pulled out a/an _____ _____,
(an adjective)   (the biggest thing you can think of)

and threw that as well.

But nothing seemed to stop the _____
(a disgusting adjective)

Commander _____!
(the gross adjective and thing you used twice on page 244)

(Draw yourself here)   (Draw the stuff you are   (Draw your evil villain here)
                            throwing through the air)

"This looks like a job for Captain Underpants!" shouted

_____ .
(your first name)

Suddenly, Captain Underpants _____
(a verb ending in "ed")

into the school. "Hi," said Captain Underpants.

"How's your _____ _____
(an adjective)   (an animal)

_____ today?"
(a part of the body)

"That doesn't make any sense," said Harold.

"Who cares?" said _____ . "We've got
(your first name)

to stop that villain!" So Captain Underpants grabbed a

baseball bat and hit Commander _____

_____ over the head repeatedly.
(the gross adjective and thing you used twice on page 244)

(Draw yourself here)   (Draw your evil villain here)

HERE COMES THE BAT, MAN!

(Draw your villain here. Make him about the same height
as Captain Underpants. If you need help, look at the
Flip-O-Ramas between pages 268 and 313 for inspiration.)

HERE COMES THE BAT, MAN!

(Draw your villain here. Make him about the same height
as Captain Underpants. If you need help, look at the
Flip-O-Ramas between pages 268 and 313 for inspiration.)

"Holy _____ _____ !" shouted
(a verb ending in "ing")   (an animal)

George. "Captain Underpants has defeated Commander

_____ _____ !"
(the gross adjective and thing you used twice on page 244)

"Let's celebrate by eating _____ servings of
(a number)

_____ and drinking _____ cups
(an adjective)   (something gross)   (a number)

of _____ _____," said Harold.
(an adjective)   (a disgusting liquid)

"That sounds delicious," said _____ .
(your first name)

"Just be sure to sprinkle some _____
(a gross adjective)

_____ on my food, and add a slice of
(creepy things)

_____ to my _____."
(something gross)   (the disgusting liquid you used above)

(Draw yourself sitting here)

(Draw your defeated
villain lying here)

250

(ANSWER ON PAGE 318)

HOW TO DRAW
WEDGIE WOMAN

1.

2.

3.

4.

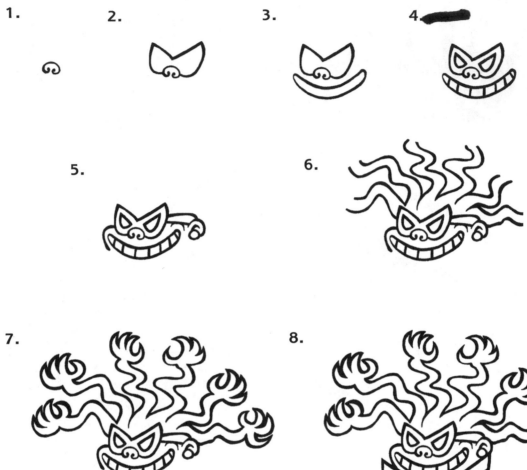

5.

6.

7.

8.

9.

10.

11.

12.

13.

14.

15.

16.

HOW TO DRAW ZORX, KLAX AND JENNIFER

1.

2.

3.

4.

5.

6.

7.

8.

9.

10.

11.

12.

13.

14.

15.

16.

FUN WITH ACCESSORIES

1. Add eyelashes!

2. Add lipstick!

3. Add a bow!

Zorxette

4a.   4b.

Klaxette

5a.

5b.

Jenniferette

6a.

6b.

(ANSWER ON PAGE 319)

(ANSWER ON PAGE 319)

Q) Why does Ms Ribble keep a stick of dynamite in her car repair kit?

A) In case she gets a flat and needs to blow up one of her tyres.

Q) Why was the mushroom always invited to parties?

A) Because he was a fungi!

Q) What's the difference between Mr Krupp and an elephant?

A) One is huge, wrinkled, has a goofy nose and smells terrible . . . and the other is an elephant!

Q) What's green, cold and topped with whipped cream?

A) A snot-fudge sundae.

Q) What's invisible and smells like bananas?

A) Monkey burps!

Q) What's the difference between pea soup and pop-corn?

A) Anyone can pop corn!

Tommy: Mummy, can I lick the bowl?

Mummy: No, Tommy, you have to flush like everybody else!

259

PRO LOG

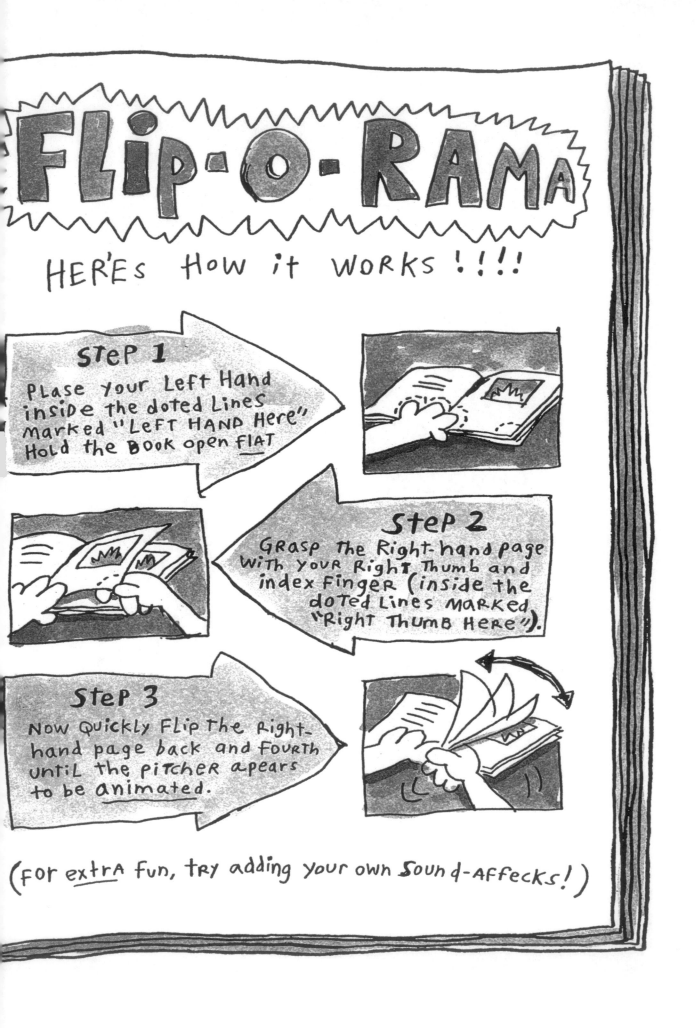

FLIP-O-RAMA 1

Pages 269 and 271.

Remember, FLip <u>only</u> page 269 while you are FLiping, be shure you can see the Pitcher on page 269 and the one on page 271.

If you FLip QuickLy, the two pitchers wiLL start to Look Like ~~two~~ <u>one</u> Animated pitcher.

Left Han
Here

Smack Attack

RIGHT
THUMB
HERE

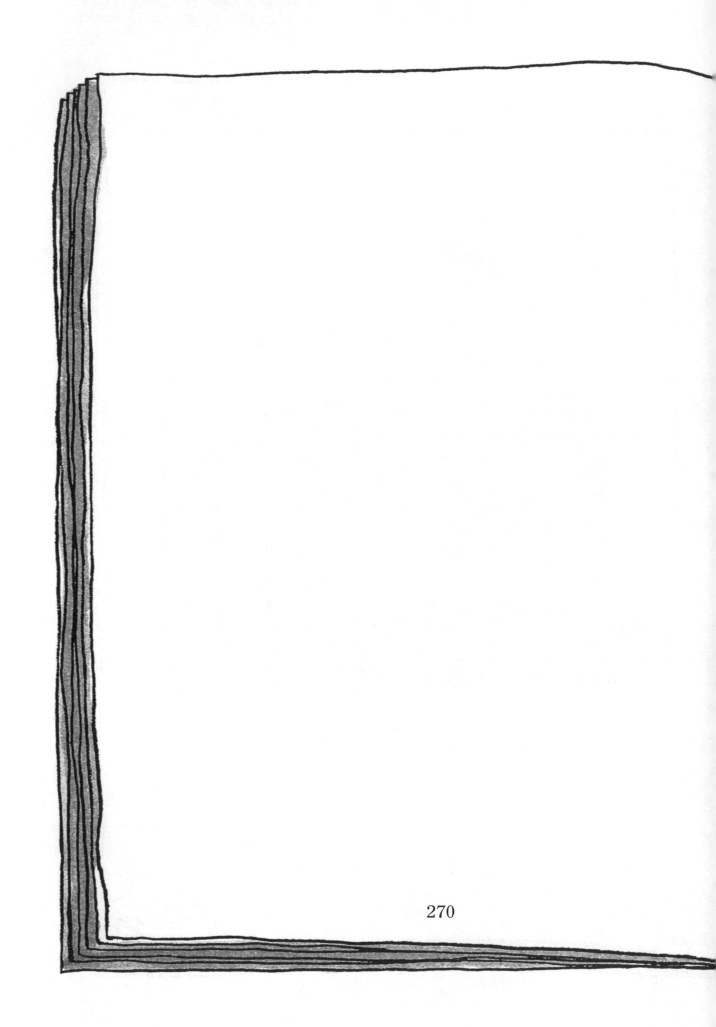

270

Smack Attack

I am woman,
see me punch

Right
thumB
Here

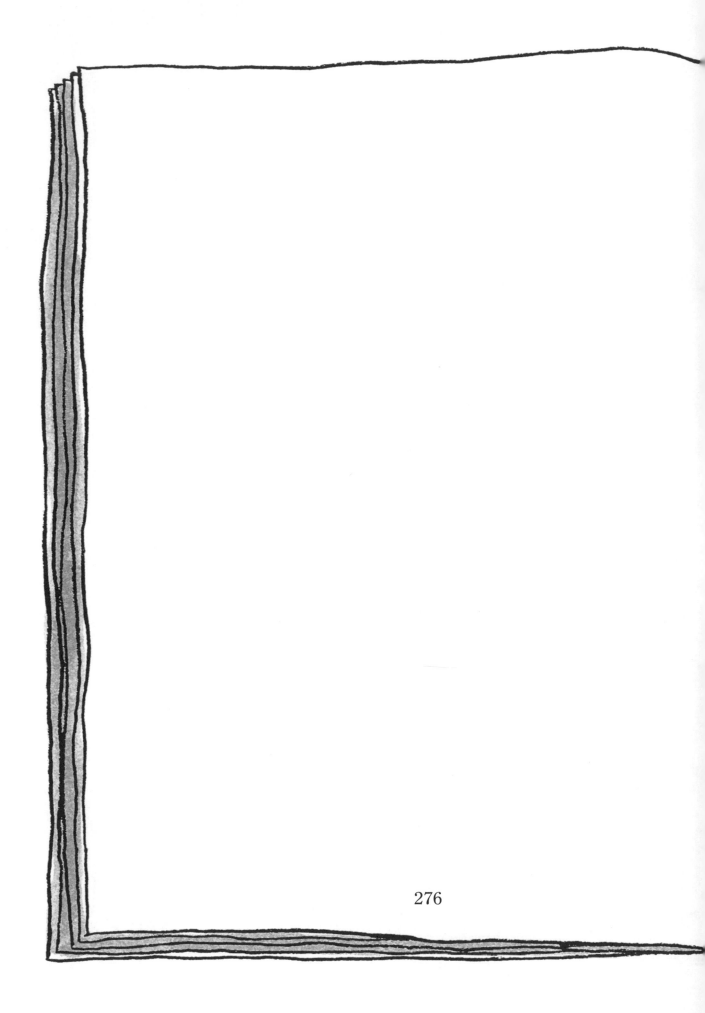

I am woman,
see me punch

With every flash, Hairy Potty morphed more and more.

...and Dr Frankenbeanies experiment grew and grew.

Welcome to the world, baby! I am your creater, and you shall obey me. You shall atend to my every wim.
Uh... master?
First, go into the kichen and wash all of the dishes. And bake me a pie while your at it. Then mop the floors and wash the windows and sow my socks and iron my pants and cook my dinner and make my bed and...
Hey master... um--- Hey master???

strechy
strechy

RIGHT
THUMB
Here

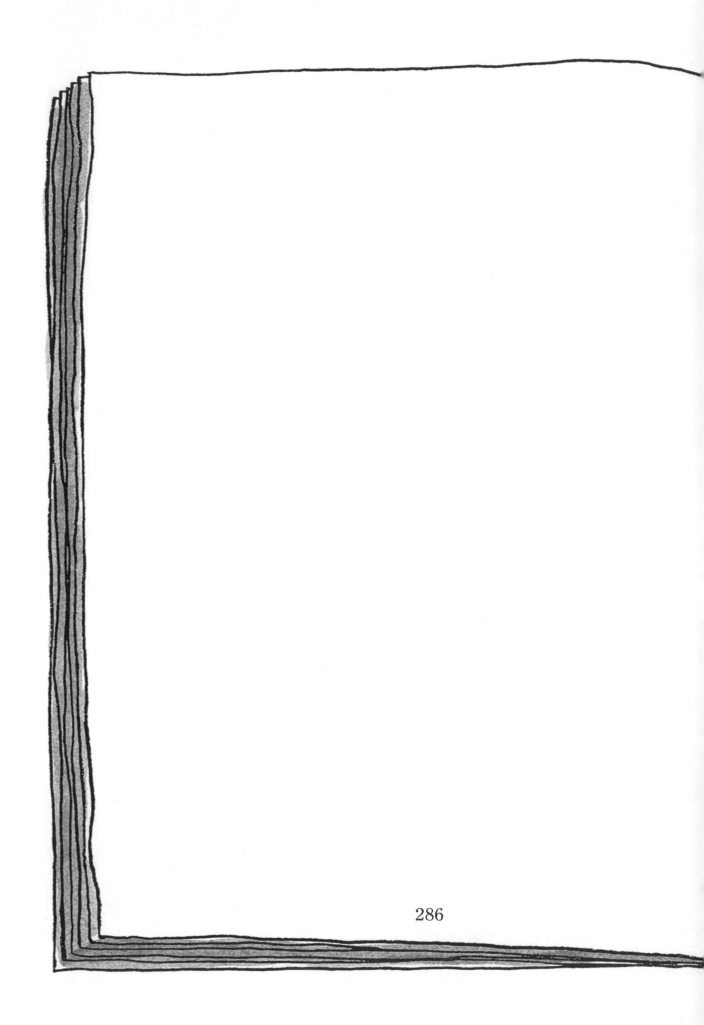

Strechy
strechy

Jumping rope
with a dope.

RiGHt
thumB
Here

290

Jumping rope
with a dope.

Hairy Potty took his new girlfrend out for a Lovley dinner of Toilet Paper and Urinel cakes.

Then it was off to vegas for a Romantic wedding
Do you take this toiLet to be your LawfuLLy wedded toiLet?
Ok.
You may now fLush the Bride
FinaLy, it was time for...
MASS DESTRUCTSiON
This Looks Like a joB For....

soon they arived at the seeen.

Quick--- We have To help him before those Toilets come to.
OK.
So Super Diaper Baby Flew Captain Underpants up to a safe plase on top of a bilding. But Diaper Dog Flew home. He had a plan...
ULP

InFLate-a-BowL

RIGHt
ThumB
Here

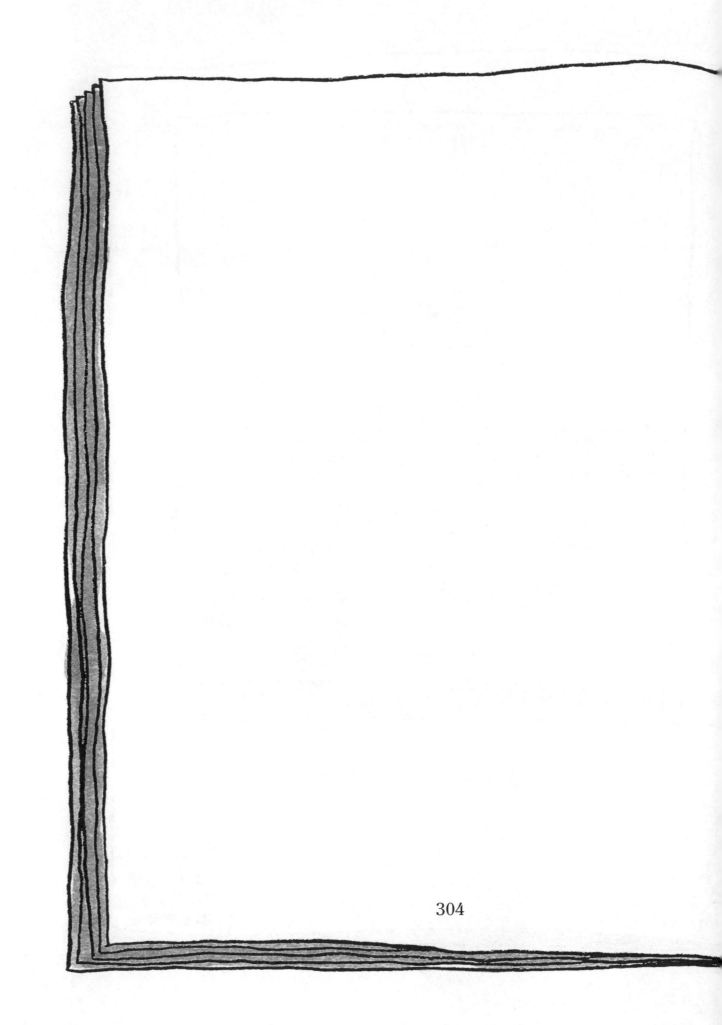

InFLate-a-BowL

Hammer time

Right
thumB
Here

312

Hammer time

ANSWERS

WORD FIND P. 229

CHART A

Benny
Billy
George
Harold
Melvin
Morty
Pippy
Tara
Tippy

CHART B

Beard
Fyde
Hoskins
Hutchins
Krupp
Poopypants
Ribble
Sneedly
Tinkletrousers

BONUS QUIZ P. 228

CROSSWORD P. 233

317

**MAZE
P. 236**

**MAZE
P. 251**

**MAZE
P. 257**

**MAZE
P. 258**